Our Fun Dad

Our Fun Dad
Copyright © 2021 by Scott Ellis
Illustrated by Jennifer Oertel

All rights reserved. No part of this book may be reproduced or transmitted in any form or by any means without written permission from the publisher and author.

Additional copies may be ordered from the publisher for educational, business, promotional or premium use.
For information, contact ALIVE Book Publishing at:
alivebookpublishing.com, or call (925) 837-7303.

ISBN 13
978-1-63132-129-0 Hardcover
978-1-63132-122-1 Paperback

Library of Congress Control Number: 2020925373

Library of Congress Cataloging-in-Publication Data
is available upon request.

First Edition

Published in the United States of America by ALIVE Book Publishing and ALIVE Publishing Group, imprints of Advanced Publishing LLC
3200 A Danville Blvd., Suite 204, Alamo, California 94507
alivebookpublishing.com

PRINTED IN THE UNITED STATES OF AMERICA

10 9 8 7 6 5 4 3 2 1

Our Fun Dad

Scott Ellis

Alive Book Publishing

To my daughters
Audrey and Kelsey
Thank you for giving me a wonderful
second childhood—yours!

Author's Note:

This book was written before my twin daughters were born with my hopes of someday being the dad my kids would brag about. My daughters and I subsequently enjoyed experiencing every scene in this book and I have been blessed with every minute of their childhood and so proud of the thoughtful and joyful young ladies they have become.

My goal for dads who receive and read this book is to have them also be bragged about by their kids and be thanked later in life for always being there for them. Please don't be the "other" dad, be the fun dad. You only get one chance at this life and whether you were always there for your kids or not, they will always remember.

My daughter Audrey passed away unexpectedly in March 2020 from Covid-related heart failure after having just graduated from nursing school. The last time we were together she hugged me and thanked me for always being there for her and for always being a fun dad. The heartbreak of losing her is indescribable yet there is healing comfort in not having the remorse and regret that I could have been there more often.

Please don't miss a single one of your kids' school plays, sporting events, birthday parties, dance recitals or bedtime stories. Even better, volunteer to coach or help whenever asked. It pays off the rest of your life. It's never too late until they are gone.

We are just like other kids
who love to laugh and play.
Our mom is just like other moms
and helps us through each day.

One of us is different,
we think you will agree.
Our silly dad is so much fun;
come on along and see!

Most dads go to work each day
and come home when they're done.
They read the mail then watch TV
and seem to have no fun.

Our dad loves to hurry home
and give us horseback rides.
He loves to have us count to ten
then find him where he hides.

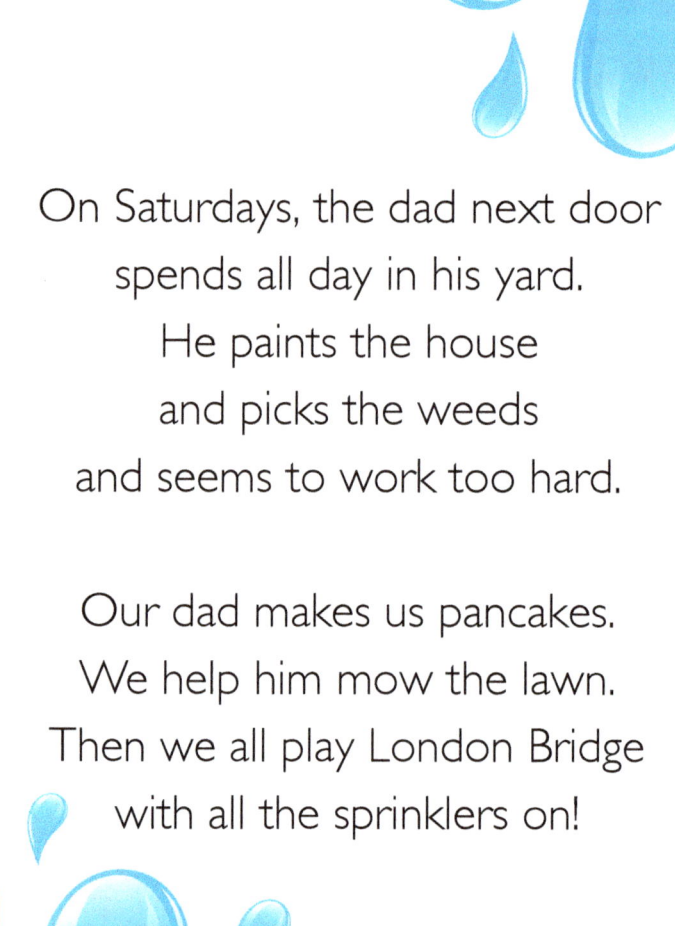

On Saturdays, the dad next door
spends all day in his yard.
He paints the house
and picks the weeds
and seems to work too hard.

Our dad makes us pancakes.
We help him mow the lawn.
Then we all play London Bridge
with all the sprinklers on!

The zoo has lots of animals;
it's fun to watch them play.
The other kids stay far behind,
their dads say "keep away."

Our dad lets us get up close
and pet the jumping seals.
We sneak up to the monkey cage
and catch banana peels.

Springtime is for baseball.
We choose up teams and play.
The other dads go golfing
every Saturday.

The games are played at our house.
No one likes to quit.
Dad kneels down and pitches,
until each kid gets a hit.

On summer days we love the pool.
The other kids do too.
Their moms and dads stay in the shade
and wear their hats and shoes.

Our dad climbs the diving board
and jumps high in the air.
He yells and does a cannonball
that splashes everywhere!

When our dad takes us camping
up to our favorite lake,
it may be past our bedtime,
but we're still wide awake.

We lie out in our sleeping bags
and one-by-one we try,
to count up all the shooting stars
across the nighttime sky.

We love to ride the carousel
on Sunday afternoons.
The other kids wave to their dads
who stand with their balloons.

Our dad climbs his favorite horse
and says "It's time to race!"
He yells and holds a carrot
down by his horse's face.

Our favorite night is Halloween.
We love to trick or treat.
The other dads just sit inside
all up and down our street.

Everybody loves our house.
Our dad makes it fun.
He wears a mask up on the roof
and scares kids one-by-one.

In winter when it rains all day
how boring can it get?
Our friends all have to stay inside,
their dads say it's too wet.

Dad wraps us up in garbage bags
and puts our rain boots on.
We stomp through all the puddles
and splash them 'til they're gone.

School nights are for homework.
It's never ever fun.
All kids have to do it.
Just sit there 'til it's done.

Our dad uses flashcards
and if we answer right,
he brings us milk and cookies
before we say goodnight!

Most kids have a bedtime
that seems to come too soon.
Their dads yell, "Go to sleep!"
from across the living room.

Our dad reads a story,
then kisses us goodnight.
We feel so safe and cozy
as he turns off all the lights.

So as we fall asleep at night
we thank our lucky stars
for all the time Dad spends with us;
we hope your dad is like ours!

ALIVE Book Publishing and ALIVE Publishing Group
are imprints of Advanced Publishing LLC,
3200 A Danville Blvd., Suite 204, Alamo, California 94507
Telephone: 925.837.7303   alivebookpublishing.com

ABOOKS

www.ingramcontent.com/pod-product-compliance
Lightning Source LLC
Chambersburg PA
CBHW040323050426
42453CB00017B/2442